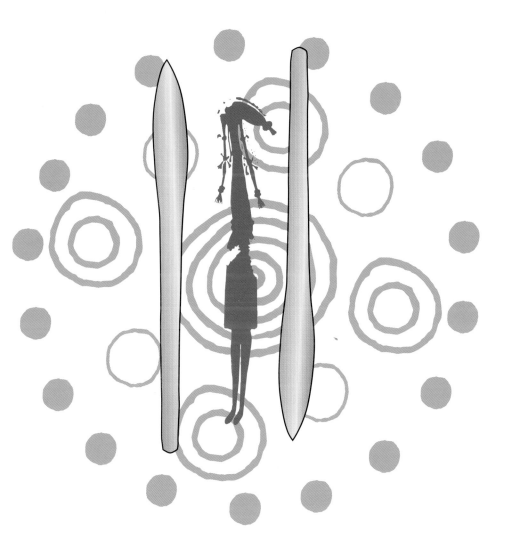

1

'Marn-grook' is a sport. You keep the ball off the ground.

'Ju-ju' is a yam stick. You can play a tag sport with 'ju-ju'.

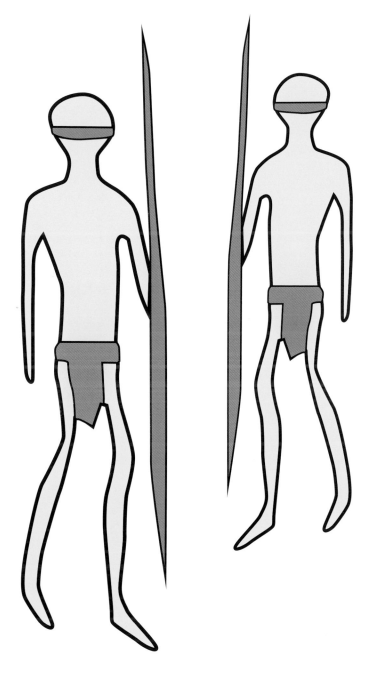

5

Bo-ya is a stone to the Noongar people. You lay out stones and run around these.

The First People were fast and strong.

'Kool -jak' was a swan to the Noongar people. This was a game of moving silently around an area.

11

'Gun-dah' is a stick game. The stick will hit the ball.

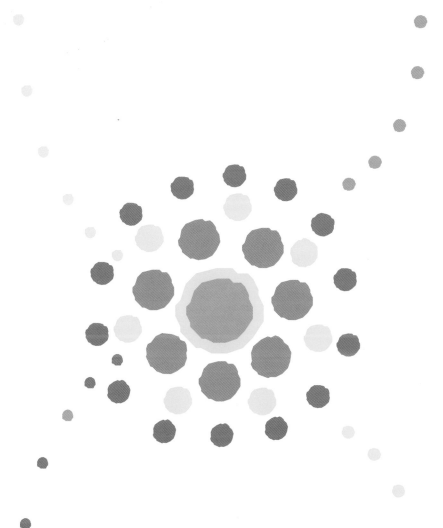

13

'Bin-gi-ing' means turtle. This game is to stop getting to the eggs.

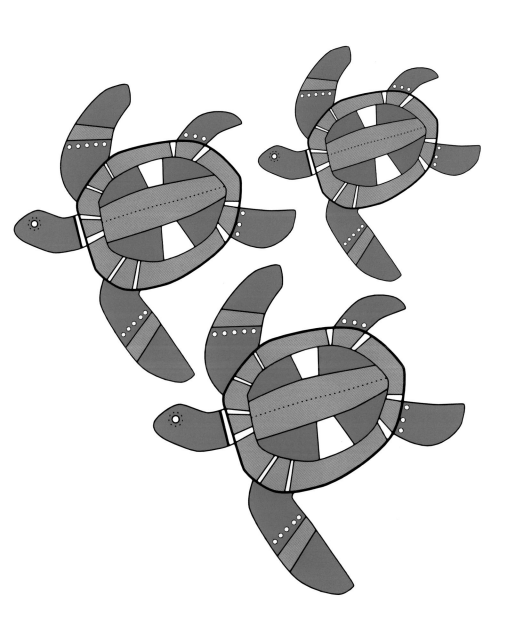

15

The First People of the desert called a stone, 'we-me'. You knock over the stick with a 'we-me'.

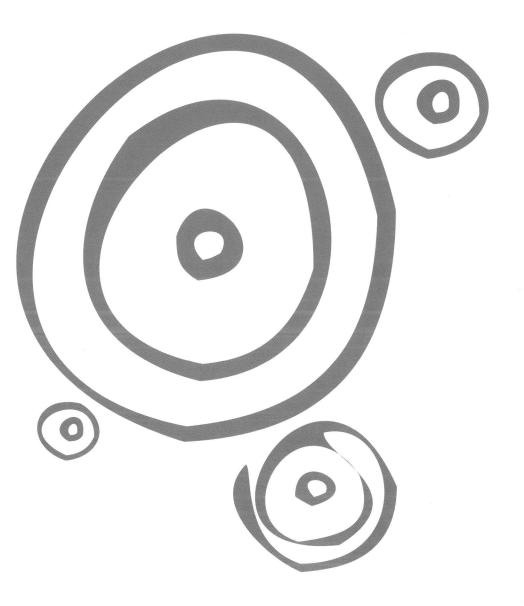

17

The 'Boo-mer-ang' is like a frisbee. It spins through the air.

19

The snake was 'Mal-ya' and the sport was a jumping rope.

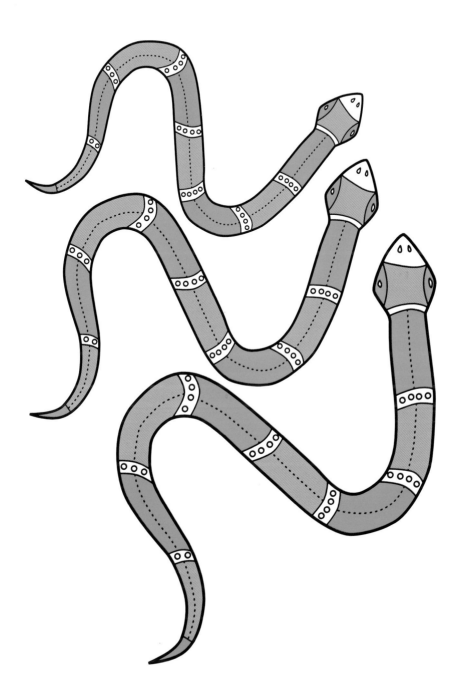

21

'Guy-ga' is the word for hunt.
This is a tag sport.

23

Word bank

Gun-dah	turtle
stick	getting
Kool-jak	Bin-gi-ing
Marn-grook	desert
sport	knock
ground	stick
yam	frisbee
stick	Boo-mer-ang
people	jumping
Noon-gar	rope
around	sport
fast	
strong	